Anarchy and Pancakes

Poems by Dan Pohl

Illustrations by Jessie Pohl

Kansas City　Spartan Press　Missouri

Spartan Press
Kansas City, Missouri
spartanpresskc.com

Spartan Press

Copyright (c) Dan Pohl, 2018
First Edition 1 3 5 7 9 10 8 6 4 2
ISBN: 978-1-946642-37-0
LCCN: 2018930971

Design, edits and layout: Jason Ryberg
Author photo: Dan Pohl
Cover image and design: Jessie Pohl
All rights reserved. No part of this publication may be reproduced or transmitted in any form or by any means, electronic or mechanical, including photocopying, recording or by info retrieval system, without prior written permission from the author.

Spartan Press would like to thank Prospero's Books, The Fellowship of N-finite Jest, The Prospero Institute of Disquieted P/o/e/t/i/c/s, Will Leathem, Tom Wayne, Jeanette Powers, j.d.tulloch, Jason Preu, Mark McClane, Tony Hayden and the whole Osage Arts Community.

Eighteen Moves to Checkmate and *Why the Drama of the Socially Puzzled* were printed in *Gimme Your Lunch Money: Heartland Poets Speak Out against Bullies* (an anthology 2016.)

Lizy Discovers Her Shadow, For Those Who Carry Water Ripples and Heirloom, and *End of Dante's Walk at the Museum of Jurassic Technology* were published in *365 Days: A Poetry Anthology by 365-Day Poets*

Gone was published in the *North Dakota Quarterly,* Volume 79, Issue 2, spring 2012 in celebration of 100 years of William Stafford, as well as in the 2015 Yearbook of The Kansas Authors Club.

Baked Potato, Summer Jazz, Climbing Style, In Memory of the Church Ladies and Reverend Bob, Gone, Lectionary of Land, and *Ease into It* were recorded to a CD called *View from Smoky Hill: It's Kansas,* volume 1,

First Spring Cut was published on *Kansas Time and Place: Poetry of Kansas Here and Now*

CONTENTS

Unpaved Roads / 1

Lectionary of Land / 2

Ease into It / 3

Monet Sky / 4

Spring Serenade / 5

Ripples an Heirloom / 6

Something about a Pond / 7

Ballad / 8

Barefoot on Summer's Sand / 9

By September Eleven, Note / 10

Fall into It / 11

Memory in Stones / 12

Gone / 13

To Get Along / 14

Summer Jazz / 15

Lizy Discovers Her Shadow / 16

Fright / 19

Sin Eater / 20

Personally Annotated / 21

Plato's Fifth Grade Allegory / 22

Abraham Met with Tears / 23

At Night, the Eaten Dead / 25

Flinch / 26

Hot Enough? / 27

The World Slows / 28

Blizzard 1883 / 29

Socrates Loved to Dance / 31

Anarchy and Pancakes / 32

Sand Spills Out / 33

Ubuntu / 34

What is the World? / 35

The Way / 36

Next Movement of Will / 37

Baked Potato / 38

First Spring Cut / 39

Too Long in Trees / 41

In Memory of the Church Ladies
  and Reverend Bob / 42

Fly, If Only Imagined / 44

Of Bones and Badgers / 45

Translation / 46

End of Dante's Walk at The Museum
  of Jurassic Technology / 48

Why the Drama of the Socially Puzzled / 51

For Those Who Carry Water / 52

Climbing Style / 55

Eighteen Moves to Checkmate / 56

That Certain Freedom / 58

July Fourth at Longview Lake / 60

Sock Monkeys / 62

Hard Stuff of Little Things / 64

What You Keep / 65

In memory of Rebecca Ann Markley Pohl

Unpaved Roads

The GPS has its own mind
Focused so much on cities
A certain perspective of
The programmer, junk in

Junk out, advice from a
Female voice, seductive
Trills of vowels, consonants
Each time I press her buttons

With the question asked of me
Your destination is on an
Unpaved road; are you
Certain you want to go there?

Yes.

Lectionary of Land

Mark it well and good, walking through seasons
Page after page, to get to harvest gatherings
With chants inside circles, and we know
    Our human moments

By what's important to us by the turn of
Hallmark's calendar that tells what card and
When, so we know about our births, our lives
    Our deaths, our moving

Waves through wheat, animated on the land
That offers us resurrection, twining through
It, recognizing its sense, its focus with time
    That shapes

The years and then a west wind, which
Breathes fire for new grasses that speak
Benedicere, the Latin long forgotten
    Sharing our life, our bread

Ease into It

Maybe, that's the way it should sound, boats sliding out
Into the water to go there, and they gently bump the others
Along the way to discover that spark that has always been
Inside, to convince them to untie their half-hitch moorings

Maybe, ease into the truth, preached by conscious poets
Of one way or that way that they know to speak together
Looking beyond their rapids in streams, the hate, the anger
The confusion, the broken ropes that have no certain grip

Maybe, you should ease into it as well, this life you found
This creation that became yours, shared with good friends
To read your movements, to interpret the signs left behind
And never judge anything so pure like another's footsteps

Monet Sky

The twilight has
The hour, the pink
End of the day,
Bold with purple
Tones that fold

Into the hush of
Too many words
Before starlight
Reveals gold,
Heavenly eyes

Shimmering,
Their passion as
Sparkles on dew,
On the soul, like
A kiss placed just

So on a long,
Fragrant nape of
Neck, the beauty
With no tears,
With no stain.

Spring Serenade

On a day   The Music

The quick Spanish strings   Will slow the shepherd's sheep
They waft a romantic air   To linger in meditative fields

A rhythm of soft chords   While lambs nibble new grass
Dance together, to spin   And frolic after small bellies fill

Love twining, twisting   Prancing the tune of life
That raises staccato spirits As bright stars watch

To fall, to rest there   As the young lie down
Silence within their joy   Evening's music in velvet ears

Ripples an Heirloom

Given in a quiet generation, a couple's
Waves start on a moonlit night, man
To woman, before the century's turn

Their lovely words still vibrate through
The families they began, vibrating like
String theory says all things tremble

Waves of light, in everyone, glow
To release the fire, one-to-one, that
We cannot see, but the rhythm builds

The rocks shake within themselves
Pressure surrendered to the earth
Well-placed to realign the world's crust

Its resonance sounds deep, rumbling
Dark amplitude, the waves volume
Welling, same sound between lovers

The heart of a jewel, a gift given years
Ago, rattles through drawers as quakes
Move within the earth, hand to hand

Something about a Pond

The pull of water in field or park
Draws those who fall deeply
Into thought, hypnotically drawn

To come pensively to shore,
The bank that beckons tired
Souls for renewal in its silence

To look into its unmoved mirror
At secondary trees and cloned
Clouds, at a reflective world

Maybe a better world, framed
By tufts of tall grass along the
Divide between a real life and

One imagined, but for which side
Of reason or which side to dream
Becomes the question during

The pitch of sticks and stones to
Ripple the surface, break the spell
And return from its offerings

Ballad

Prairies burn in festive dance
Licking flames to hum the tune
That speaks between brittle grass

    Sung by Meadowlark's whispered trill

Heard through Flint Hills' blessed tone
Its tortured soul, her heat-split wind
Smoke fills the land where cattle live

    So near in history, the bloody streams

In state, the wind has cooled to ease
Across the land's quiet, sleepy heart
A love brought from mother to child

    Healing here among bright stars

Barefoot on Summer's Sand

My heart, gray bark surrounds it
A tree, one lonely tree on an island
A tuft of grass that stands as a ghost

        Alone

On a keel of a sand dune ship to bleach
My bones, cooked in high noon's light
To become one isolated oxygen isotope

        There

To vibrate above the silicate ground on
Which I stand, circled by hugging heat
Of the blond garden and goo of stones

By September Eleven, Note

Framing old sheds, growing out
Of electric fence lines, moving
To the road's gentle shoulder

Bush sunflowers live one bright
Moment then brown the fifteenth
The death will loosen their teeth

Seeds fall last of spring as wheat
Stubble blonds to gray, blooms
For last rites with a lowering sun

The compass arms hug the air
Like Goddess Kali, life and death
Beauty and ugliness, one package

Of Hindu philosophy, and on each
Delicate hand rests an amber ring
Petals, given by no other god but her

To fade with the very last of summer's
Heat for some to think it a noxious weed
Those who manicure their pristine ditch

Fall into It

We have time and time enough to dream and dream
To wake from so much noise, hypnotic fuzz, the world's

Electronic waste of TV Mike talking to Willy, free from
Film fog, the distracting fog of function, misplaced

To appear to the point of seeing potholes mankind
Created for itself, mental malware for sure; illusions

Fill them, falling into them, a heavy bump to shake
Teeth, to flap the cheeks, working into a busy nothing

Unable to find a good book to sit and read instead or
A bit of parchment on which to write an original thought

Or to talk and share that thought rather than watching
The loop of loops of feedback signals that cross across

Galaxies to show the lights that move in the dark night
Sky how this world has decided, by its wisdom, to think

Memory in Stones

Written in memory of the William Stafford Celebration,
Washburn University, 31 March 2014, Topeka, Kansas

During the Kansas Celebration, one-hundred
Years of sharing himself, Bill would certainly
Muse, *This is how it's done: I bring stones,*
Some full or cryptic writing and dense worlds

From my life and lighter ones to the shore
For choosing, and you bring yours as well,
Clacking in deep pockets, to share with me.
I prefer we meet where the river whispers

To toss our stones across the life of it, and
As we do, count the skips each makes over
The surface, before our stories sink into it,
To collect there from the time we shared.

Gone

Social beings need a time alone, if lucky, to retain
Some sense, some dignity, by walking a country road
At sunset, away from the manmade noise of public
Distractions, to dance within the sound steps of gravel

And sand, pushed aside, peaked in the middle
By slow cars that agree to keep down choking dust
Posted by the signs both ways near a single house
Isolated on purpose behind the hidden line spoken
By human words of the owner, *No Trespass,* which

Means nothing to the bristled terrier other side the
Gate, vanishing to gone over the cattle guard, never
Never to return, ignoring the light of the whistle to
Do so, diving into a grass sea to attack rabbit runs

To Get Along

The slope falls at thirty-five degrees
    Gliding out con-caved to zero the end
        Of each run that waits for children
            Who come out after snows on the
                Twenty-first to stand top of the hill
                    To watch their father's ploughs play
                With city loaders and dump trucks
            To clear the ten inches off streets
           To bring back their old civilization
        Their version, its forward movement
As the snow blowers and shovels of
    Have and have nots do the same
        And who go so far to find the hidden
            Sidewalk's concrete and where
                It ends at the neighbor's property line

                Oh, they wake early to become the first
            Down to flatten the crystal diamonds to
        Cream white runs for a unified theory of
        A bell curve that works with all members
Of the socio-economic where some use
    Waxed cardboard to travel, some use blue
        Molded plastic discs, purchased at Wal-
            Mart at the door, and, usually, one brings
                A Cadillac of toboggans, a Flexible Flyer
                  Red-lettered and metal railed for
                    The same opportunity at a turn

Summer Jazz

A standard peppered among triple heartbeat sets;
Some Coltrane calms the energy; the buzz between
Each improvised bell curve arraignment lifts the crowd
To charge its spirit by electrochemical art; then it
Brings them back by soft cushions of quieter notes,

> But they don't ever return to their start, not really,
> Transported a little higher by five beats per measure

Of masters with nothing to prove, who help assembled
Souls lose themselves for a while through a theory
Built skillfully with the silence between notes from well-
Worn instruments, played beyond their range of color
To discover hidden continents of sound seldom heard

> By our kind who revel in a dark, spot-lit room where
> People can discover how to breathe, so they do not

Disappear, as long as Yoder's drums pound out gray smoke,
Pisano's top-heavy sax sings whatever it wants, so clear that
Colorado spring water from the source is its only friend, and
Markley's blessed piano, played with two minds; the right
Strikes the keys sure and deep, part metronome, a guide

> For other hearts to unite them, who need its care, and
> The left lets his fingers run lightning fast to vanish.

Lizy Discovers Her Shadow

It jumps
To her excited side
Runs into stationary walls
Over the moving
Picket fence

Outside
On the flat driveway
Over the dog, at her discovery
Melts onto them like
Black butter

She tries
To touch her companion
On a bright day, that slides away
At odd angles, a jester's
Joke

Attached
At her feet, the long arms
Wave largess hands, a bold
Shameless, unapologetic
Dark shade

Finally, it does not move
Dies as she falls, a skydiver
Onto soft grass that catches her
Exhausted after chasing it
All day

Fright

Under cover of darkness, cloaked under a full-moon,
It feels good to climb an elm for ambush in shadow
One branch at a time on Halloween, a night of
Mischievous spirits, careful to solve the blind maze
By touch and monkey for the second fork to wait.

Street lights bookend the silent block of hidden,
Guarded houses, which sleep behind black-iron gates
And dark high hedges; the corners flutter with nervous
Moths, swimming forever in their dull yellow light.

Stealth, for the moment, withholds a growl, the location
Perfect for a scare to change smiles and high-pitch
Chatter behind ballerina masks, from under hobo hats,
Incognito, to tip the dominoes, shaken with no courage.

Blurred little legs arrow away from the death-filled
Scream toward the safe corner glow. Treats spill their
Trail, pointing straight to the monster that would
        Eat them if they stayed.

Sin Eater

Who throws down cash today for someone to
Swallow a three course meal of a bad life, worthy

Of it, that held no courage, no hope, no joy—only
Greed, the fire that burns inside, an anatomy of

Swindle and lies, filled with morose thoughts,
Saved by an eater of sins, a singular profession

Like grave digger or life guard with hired wailing
Mourners paid in full for the soul in front of them?

The tears cost extra; an ancient practice committed
To protect the deceased who has no desire to wander

The valley, fearing evil that he caused, purchasing
Paradise at hand, prepared and served in a well-lit

Room, a full spread with aperitifs between each
Forgiving plate in order to clear a delicate pallet.

Personally Annotated

Old, dusty, naked books call to me
At table sales, mismatched, out of
Volume; I search for those few
    With which people spoke.

They read rough, slapped with written
Liniment, rubbed onto aged skin
Pages for others to discover, their
    Thoughts from cryptic notes.

Their small lectures brand the margins
With twists of words to invite a reader
To rethink, argue with, or expand upon
A play of a shaman's lodge journey into
The soul, dead, centuries past, a deep
Resurrection, a reward or ministry for
Those in the great parade of human
    Belief or doubt.

Plato's Fifth Grade Allegory

She asked once, and I fell
Transformed as easily
As a metronome counts;
The minutes, too short
For recess, placed me into
A deep hypnotic state by
The sway she carried
Through the arc, hands
To hips on friendly terms,
To push the fresh smell
Of her, a new scent to
Ponder at the swings.

The chains, the seat,
The breeze from her travel,
Her smile, the soft sand
Below, the deep blue sky
Above, the minutes melted
Away and created me
A martyr, happily bullied
By the high monks
On top monkey bars
Scolded at my return
But I could not.

Abraham Met with Tears

I

The truth now that too young a boy should attach to
Poems, while grief fills empty space among letters,
Passed from a world, forever placed from his home.
He remains a time traveler thrown into phrases,
Word greased gears, running on mortal twists
                          Of all too human keys.

II

The town of Chapman gathers its dead beneath Indian
Hill among old cedars, so old their resin fills the air.
Could we find a happier end other than his death,
Surrounded by living trees? Dare we stretch lifeless
Tendons if we could? His hand leaves unclasped his
Mother's brown hair; for him, life comes too late to live,
Too late to grow, and our forges fire weak flames, too weak
To open brown eyes given to evergreens keeping their guard
Through centuries, to whisper for him using breezes
From the valley, and to wrap their watch around
                          His small stone.

At Night, the Eaten Dead

Did the crystal skull say something or do sock
Monkeys slide passed black corners or under
    Safe, high beds?

What about the happy clown sitting in the chair?

My shadows have red lips for kissing the life
From innocence and blood back asses as they
    Leave their victim.

In the dark, the moon smiles too late to help.

Who is it who giggles from stealth in that dark?
Hours speak by growl in dreadful dreams, a slow
    Wet place,

The itch of goose bumps, raised flesh, shaken.

Children never wanted the broken shards of fear,
Where nighttime puppets keep their secret pull
    So quiet,

 Whose look promised parents their good love.

Flinch

Silently, the edge of the back porch roof
Sires one wet and sloppy-cold droplet to
Hang there by one cautious digit, a tear

> Of Kansas rains, forming in anguish on
> A crystal dawn after the night's anger

And rage of grinding winds, complaints of
Flash photography, as if some star came out
One bolt after another, landing, striking close
> To feel their heavy heat

Shaking quiet, gentle people from their
Deep dreams by rasping reports and high
Screams through trees' fingers that could

> Not catch their fear, moaning sounds
> Of pitched banshees, shaken old putty

From pane's bones for that moment when
It releases its cold spit toward terminal
Velocity that slaps the open eye to blink

Hot Enough?

Walk northeast long enough, the journey
Will end someplace over the rocky cliffs of
Labrador before falling into the cold, deep
Atlantic where the Canadian natives will tell
People to forget what they know about the
Weather in May, June, and July

It's difficult to read the season with
So much snow and icy fog, the frozen ground
A frigid dream; a stranger comes with memory
Of a distant land, the heated heartland,
The states stacked one upon the other
Where farmers burn stubble across their faces,
Creating manmade storms and twisting fire and
Smoke, gray and white, like Tristan and Iseult
Dance; her skirts billow and glide across the
Highways and blacktop county roads to hurt
Drivers' teary eyes for want of closing vents
Or killing air conditioners, running through
      Dark clouds as vaporous ghosts

The ruin rises into the sky, creating flaming
Orange tornadoes that whirl across the roasting
Ground, like the giants that dervish without care
Over the angry face of a boiling sun

The World Slows

When trees rattle with their iced skin
Or the Rose of Sharon's spines crack
With frozen tears, how can you sleep

When their sounds peal the night
By winds that stick their tongues to
Clacking bark, complaining in tempo

And pitch after they cross the line to
Become maracas or rain sticks, cold
Enemy of bees and chilly horses that

Hide themselves in dark hives and closed
Barns, as frigid air breathes passed them
Praying the way they do for morning's

Sun, speaking to those who drive like
Old people walk on ice; care-filled eyes
Move west, coming close to wrecking

From a peek in the rearview mirror
At frozen light on trees, grass, captured
To push sights that make angels tremble

Blizzard 1883

I
As spiritual beings, people adore the sun, passionate
For its visits, worshipers, so small, who itch for its fire.

II
Before the old century's turn, a root cellar door, bare
Wood, gray and weathered over the years, near the
Washhouse, opened heavy with pushing snow: the
Pair, flame touched ghosts, welcomed the morning's
Jacinth sun.

Drifts wedged onto the living and the dead, ten feet in
Places, scooped around split cottonwoods, cedars, and
Splintered sheds, scream touched by hi-pitched banshee
Cries that knifed through the central prairie with mortal
Sighs.

Their cattle had drifted with the wind and would not
Return; the pigs and chickens could not breathe from
Thick, harsh pounding powder, moving in waves made
From winds, such winds that scythed through darkness
Unlit by living stars, to frighten them to cling to each
Other for silence.

Countless diamonds radiated their features from below,
Lifting them as if they walked on pure light; each step held
A moment then fell to stamp shadows of their movement
As they danced and circled each other above it all.

Socrates Loved to Dance

At thirty, he drank
His death, his price
To cause concern
With the powerful
Who did not take
To an examined life
For the deep spoken
Embarrassment of
The unimpressed
Few did know
How he loved to
Dance with wild
Abandon, out of
Character for the
Well-seasoned
Thinker, while
Every softened
Part of his body
Moved in time with
Rhythmic songs

Anarchy and Pancakes

One water drop
>> Skitters across
>> Sizzles to death
>> Its hum and ping
>> Glides above
>> A microscopic
>> Field of steam
>>> Kissing untouched
>>> Metal, the grill
>>> Hot enough
>>>> For pancakes

The word, one
>> Word slides
>> Onto a page
>> To trap itself
>>> Face up to wait
>>> Patiently for
>>> Its discovery

With potential
>> Power, stored
>> Energy, the quiet
>> Frozen accent
>> Watches through
>> Time, sits still
>> An impression
>> Nothing more
>> Until the world's
>> Anarchy calms
>>> Enough to notice

Sand Spills Out

*We are only earthenware jars that hold
this treasure, to make it clear that such
an overwhelming power comes from
God and not from us.* –2 Cor. 4:7

The pot breaks, in time it does
To release its content, a damp
Course sand mixed with rich dirt
What's inside, put there by faith

Released in time, like people
Want, and that is your life, its
Center; the ideas run through
It like sand that never joins in

Cannot by its nature to find its
Own level as water does, just
Slower in flow to live in place
Where in hindsight you should

Ubuntu

> *Umuntu ngumuntu ngabantu.* –Zulu Maxim

A person is a person through other people,
An African shaman would say and agree that
People cannot, must not, exist in isolation, like
John Donne thought, heard through centuries
      On the old savannah.

One evening in June when Venus passed before
The sun, I read a serendipitous wire of a word,
An electric cord of a word, an introduction, body,
And conclusion in one word—interconnectedness,
A singular essay for humanity and its many woes.

This rope of a word could stand as constitution
And founding document as the world ends this
Mayan age, if anything, to stop the supernatural
Practice of spontaneous invisibility while standing
In line as others push passed without noticing
      A person already there.

What is the World?

Finally
    Choice
        Will
            Define
    The symbol
        The world
            As symbol
                This present
                    World into
        The
            Cheese
    Puff
        Air-filled mostly
    Satisfying crunch
  Little nutrition
  Fattening
Oh, high vibratory taste   Salty
    Vivid color
        Day-Glo
            Yellow-orange
                That sticks to fingers
            Produced
        With little money
    The bottom line
Sold
    For more
        Than it's worth

The Way

Today, as mankind struggles with the age
And ego, battling powers inflict wounds
By callous drones, watching, observing to spy

Upon embedded souls, planted by force
Or family, yet the people will remember
In the end, how hard stones crumble, broken

By soft rains and warm thoughts that move
Across the waves of Kansas hills and fields
And under pastures rests a holy sea for

The difficulties the land has always known
Carved by the slow arms of mighty glaciers
So long ago, shaping, sculpting that which

Understands, to heal, to forgive, amending
The wrong when it comes to it, finally, to pick
The right way, our way, the one we know

Next Movement of Will

In the East, a child sleeps
    Dreams undisturbed
In the West a mother's joy wakes
    On a sun-filled morning
And a quiet train moves through
    The land at peace, in peace
After a time of no thought
    Mankind now wills
Not to live in error so long disputed
    By bodies
The names that died, unforgotten
    We lift them as saints
For a path we found—fearless, rejoicing
    Blessed for once by humbleness
In character and a certain caring
    A passion
Beyond the wounds, the hurts
    The wicked death
That has followed until this moment
    To take roads home
Confident, rolling deep with knowing rains
    In hills
With the distant bells of pasture cattle
    That always knew how

Baked Potato

Don't you know love comes from creation
Loaded will work from the garden, grown
For me to mash and smash and mix to an
Almost soup in its own brown bowl, but

It takes time, with eyes that laugh at its
Doom, choked by clarified butter and bacon
Bits to bring out its spirit, like slicing into an
Angel's heart, fried chicken just a side and

Nothing special, as sour cream slathers
On the worship by the silverware, knife
And fork with some heft, dancing to make the
Drippings fall over the edge; their rain arcs

Across its earthly skin, straight from dirt, for
Me to pray and prick and gourmet taste, eyes
Up, *My God, that's good!* after a dash of
Course black pepper for heaven's best gift

First Spring Cut

First cut of two-week spring growth
Shows a maze of field mice runs
Exposed to keen barn owls and
Hungry hawks that leer for any sign

Of a sneeze of movement to release
A Pandora's Box of hurt from above
Yet last year's tall turf keeps their lives
Near the cemetery, where the dead

Have a place outside town from attack
While raiding cut maize and corn rows
For released, forgotten seeds that fell
From summer, daily destinations

As is the pasture's pond nearby
So their trails connect by Y's like
Family trees branch, webs of roads
Roofed by rasping straw when wind

Exhales across the tunnels, as crooked
As Russian rivers, paths stamped to
Bare earth by quick pads of paws, as
If Greek music plays, scurrying beats

Of feet each day to socials in burrows
While at night they cuddle in warmth
Covered and tucked-in to sleep under
Such grass, in order to forget the sun

Too Long in Trees

The Great Pyramid
Means nothing to
Cousins who stood
Down from family
One mark removed
    Unable to finish
    Nor would want to
    Their gene joke
    The punch line

Perhaps they met
In some forgotten ape
Council and found too
Much trouble evolving
For their lazy efforts
Howling in green canopies
    They gather
    Tasty edibles
    Love and sleep
    Live the moment

What luxury as each
Carries one worried thought
    Last time I smelled that
    It tried to eat me

In Memory of the Church Ladies and Reverend Bob

In the Sheds
> Like animals, they find it hard to wait
> For their daily corn and feed meals—
> Gladys, Bea, and Helen—while the
> Honorable Reverend Bob sniffs them
> From his shed two doors down, sows
> In heat but hungry and uninterested
> In his needs, Maslow's hierarchy in its
> Place about what's important, to dance
> Around the grain and each other, grinding
> It up by molars, complaining out loud

With grunting tongues

In the Pasture
> At his end, Reverend Bob costs more than
> He's worth, and Bea has turned bully
> Knocking Stephen down as he sprints
> Each day to fling and spread their vitamin
> Enriched food before them, moving fast
> Stepping like a water-walking Jesus lizard
> In beat-up, tan work boots, most times
> Winning, sometimes not, lucky to regain
> His footing as their radar pings the target

Then he decides

In the End
> No more piglets remain and Bea rests in the
> Freezer; cash cuddles in Stephen's new jean's
> Pocket to buy his safe retirement to ferment
> Beer, feeding yeast, small critters that eat his
> Sugar, a sweeter life, instead of two o'clock
> Birthing that interrupts his sleep, taking him
> From his warm comfort on winter mornings
> But now, the livestock eats through the night
> And he happily sips gold, making more money
> In one than he did in eighteen years with the
> Swine to tell stories with more friends about
> Their doom and his luck to still have his life

Uneaten

Fly, If Only Imagined

Ten-pound filament descends as
A whisper into a gentle pasture
Moved by soft, warm breezes
Pierced between two dragon eyes
That hunger to hunt for prey below

The thin, coiled serpent rides high
Lashed upon crossed wood braces
        Blood scales twist the tail
          Cupped onto curved balsa

The beast hunts resting cattle below
Cows as islands, unmoved, watching
Golden waves of grass break upon
Their content yet cautious shores

Of Bones and Badgers

The saints rise from graves again
The ones who did not need protection
From evil and its decay to ashes, who

Rest together in rotten-wood caskets
Of crumbling pine put down into the
Ground the legal six feet; clever claws

Dig and scatter gnawed bones across
The church lawn onto the prairie, left
Tribute from an upturn of the natural

Order, out of place, the law broken
With a soup of souls placed beyond

Safe sleep, interchangeable parts of
Digits and joints of elders after fierce
Excavation for collection in a box, not

Knowing which piece belonged to whom
For a short ceremony then reburial in the
Corner, fifth spot in line, listed by date

Translation

It is time for cats to
Develop opposable
Thumbs, in order to

Grow a speech center
In their feline brains
To become aware of

Their passing into history
And to understand that
They have one; then they

Could create a cat
Government, better than
Ours and a cat religion

That worships old Egyptians
I suppose, or learn to write
With their opposable

Thumbs, poetry, on what
They thought about while
They sat in curtained windows

Those years or hung by one paw
Caught on screen doors, to leave
A part of themselves

In creation after their
Deliberate
Evolution

End of Dante's Walk at The Museum of Jurassic Technology

I
Embedded displays, spiral stair cases
Seven behind glass in the well's wall
Offer different designs of the same
Form above the handrail moving up
From dungeon's belly of a far journey

II
The beast below, dark and maze riddled
With no certain feel of place or direction
Each room filled with confusing sights
Each room leading into another at odd
Turns of corners and dead ends, like a
Library that suddenly appeared, a better
Lighting for some hope from the darker
Displays of microscopic art that fits, sits
In eyes of needles and small dioramas
Of desert trailers or the small entrance
Of a long-dead drive-in theater, boxed

III
However, climbing Victorian carpeted
Stairs closer to Beatrice and heaven,
The air became cool, sweet somehow
Different from the high humidity sweat

From the journey, its long progression
To a Middle East tea room, Turkish
Maybe, after learning the acquired art
Of contemplation by thinking through
Intricacies of cat's cradles for the heart
To relax with the tea then, sitting on rich
Damask cushions and taking time to
Take time to notice another elevation

IV
Sorrowful notes of a violin came from
A vestibule up short steps that climbed
Into an open-roofed reflection garden
That welcomes with echoes of water
The sad sound of melancholy music
Changed to a brighter tune as sandals
Touch the top tread to follow souls
Lucky to not fall back into the familiar
Earth, descending to the gloomy pit of
What was known, what was lonely lived

V
Oh, to look up and see white Imari doves
Sitting first in cages set into the garden's
Walls; next, the eye wanders to small
Ledges above, life balancing on inner
Framed shelves, impressions, refined
Standing art, busts of wisdom's women,
Tiny urns, to discover a grotto inset

Other side of the gravel-pathed garden
A destination to explore and peek passed
Its opening to discover two cages, one
Large, decorative, another demure, simple
But each held setting doves like delicate
Crafted china until they moved, a head
A wing, slightly, to reveal two guarded
Eggs to each and after the knowing, go

VI

Its space, big enough to whisper across
Heard soft words said in trusting speech
Four converging walks, the four gentle
Softer breezes, graveled, allowed steps
To speak like spirits to them, succulent
Plantings and flowering bushes to their
Living sides to hypnotize an unexpected
Calm, yet above it all, seven white linen
Sheets, rowed, span across, draped
Held horizontal by wooden rods
For the fabric to droop slightly, one last
Barrier to physical life before a traveler
Could leave the world, light into blue sky
For doves to sit, wait, and bare witness

Why the Drama of the Socially Puzzled

*Mean as a man who tells his children
that Santa Claus is dead.* —Anonymous

Mean as a bully stripping wallpaper
From the inner room of the soul, its
Spirit dispirited, the cold unneeded
In the center of social demolition
It takes only derision, snobbish in
Tone when said out of mouth with
No lock on self-control; then, to leave
A friend walks away, no explanation
Evil as good, misunderstanding, little
Said to explain what's wrong by a
Snake, villain, bitter people who do
Not speak to know the missing piece

For Those Who Carry Water

Waiting
At a rail crossing, in dangerous
thought, the world at deer rut
The flickering makes me realize
A train passes, the cross bars
Down

The wheels
Click the tracks
Like a pocket watch pendulums
On a chain, shadow to light
To shadow
The cars go by

I see myself
In a coastal village of Mexico
Watching the men gut their sea
Catch; they salt and sun-dry
Their fish by day, and I watch
The women

Make clay
Water pots that they slip and
Fire, a dozen at a time, with dry
Dead wood found along the beach
Piled around the jars and fired
To carry water from the village well

The men
Will wash and put on
Loose white shirts for the evening
The married men dance with their wives
The young men court, with sweet words
The daughters

Who carried the water home
And of the men who sold
The sun-dried fish to the boat
That came to buy them, there was one
Who thought to take it, away, and
Asked, *Where will I go?*

Climbing Style

Abandoned five-story grain elevators, ghosts of
Building silos that gave temporary storage, the
Square kind, outside old towns near train tracks
> Before there was a town that materialized
> During the 1890s, clapboard with pressed-tin
> Plates for fancy, its façade had the last breath

Of its blue paint scoured over the years by Kansas
Storms, blasted with road sands by high winds, so
Much weather, they have a way of attracting mice
> And children strong enough to think themselves
> Immortal to explore them, to climb to the top
> House and look through the windows they broke

Into the countryside for miles and pretend to fly like
Hawks or eagles, promising themselves that they
Would eat raw meat if they must to fly when they
> Reincarnate after they die, climbing the crossed
> Grid-work of rods inside that held the walls for
> The weight of phantom wheat that pushed them

Placed at intervals, up every three empty feet
Thinking themselves too apt to slip and fall and
If they did, to come back even as small birds that
> Eat salty, sourer bugs, as long as they could fly
> And to keep their climb secret, or, if not, killed
> By mothers who would if they ever found out

Eighteen Moves to Checkmate

As a new kid
Untethered to one town
I followed my father's life
Construction of dams and roads
That ran across Kansas
I-70, Ellis to Leavenworth
Took eight years, and
With each move
I would evaporate as smoke does
Like I was never there
So why make friends
Just to leave them
All that time and energy
To cry goodbye
Isolated
A Russian novelist
Self-caged in a small upper room
With a writer's fear
To fill eight-hundred blank pages
Yet wolves know the smell
Of prey's blood
And I cannot find enough wine
To clear my invisible ledger
That holds little profit
Of friendships

Adding the compound interest
Of villains like in Dickens' novels
Tacked to memory
Unable to erase the derisions
That began at their city limits
Who made newcomers feel
Like a Peanuts character
Alone in the outfield
Worried by their words
And often Goliaths fought my David
Never knowing
Like they did
What was fair
What was right
I asked where the good kids hid
Wondering why they could not find me
From the first or second moment
There among the rat bastards
Who stole their fathers' cigarettes
Drank their mothers' liqueur
And me
Feeling homesick
For someone gentle

That Certain Freedom

Silence brings up nothing
A danger to careful souls
But others find themselves
Captured in a planned play
With all the props and acts
Of actors, crying, laughing
Taking their picnic place once
Each year to remember; their
Minds wander a *fait accompli*
A communion of sorts with
Small embellishments through
The busy day, Fourth of July
Weekend, hearts that ride
The wings of smoke, eating
Good lives by hotdogs and
Dillons fried chicken, an
Easy fix, that leads them in
The sharing of baked beans
And noodle salad to get to
The cold, wet watermelon
In the evening's twilight into
Dark, saying what they have
Always said as colored shells
Argue with the night's sky as
Four-year-old Renee steals
Cousin kisses between reports

July Fourth at Longview Lake

To entertain as the Roman's did
To arouse and electrify the people
The holocaust moved through
Frightful flames to rumble thunder
Across the valley from boom and

    Doom of mortar shells, sounding

Curtains of percussion, throwing
Vibrant sheets of falling sparks
White to red, green to blue, purple
Into yellow bees that zip and
Sizzle, flying from their summer

    Flowers, leaving smoke signals

From their death of incendiary
Morse code, dot to dash from
Loud reports that glow one
Moment onto flashbulb faces
Blinking, each in the jury to

    Gently judge by quick comment

Oh my, That's pretty, Nice one
Sitting on lawn chairs after supper
In the dark to scan the night while
Unseen ashes fall to the water that
Silently eats the cremation from

    The empty, blackboard sky

Sock Monkeys

Miles of purple-topped turnip fields
Circled a five-year-old farm boy, who
Better understood from the year before
The concept for getting gifts
    He waited for the slow taste of the
    Taffy drawn Noel, months for days

His grandmother presented them
Three sock monkeys, Christmas Eve
    They sat silently under his tree, garroted
    With silken orange and brown bows
    Left over from last year's after sales

Pinned white paws covered tiny
Apelike ears, eyes, and mouths
    Such a clever girl at sixty-three
    She still shared mischief enough
    With grand gifts lovingly stitched

Unfastened, their stuffed, out stretched arms
Beckoned, and their unblinking black button eyes
Punctuated wide red-lip smiles, shivering him
    Their evil purpose watched for
    Warmth, they waited for comfort
    Patient for innocence to snuggle

Lovingly given, their soft cuddles
Turned unholy to betray a love,
An illusion, mean and ghoulish
> The purgatory puppets changed
> At night, a second time

Sleep animated, they pulled and slid their
Mute victim, paralyzed, into unspeakable
Places: dark treasured closets, dusty under-
Beds to devour him, never to return home

Desperately, he placed his fire truck, wooden
Blocks and rocking horse, guardians to bar
The terror, cherished friends, he thought, who
Turned traitorous and easily stepped aside

Until April rains came, her grandson
Listens at night, open eyed, as enfolding
Breezes sifted through the rusted porch screen
> As night thickened its sounds, he knew
> He heard three faint whispers sigh
> *He's ours!*

Hard Stuff of Little Things

Fixed in memory, more heart than head, looking into
The crystal of a poetic dusk, beyond the day's gung-ho
Of too many climbing, medieval minor kings, pejorative
Wannabes, and offended, pretending queens, beyond

Their part of unwelcome and pushy moves across
Manipulative checkered-past chessboards, a full moon
Gently peeks into the bedroom window as a friendly
Nightlight with no ego and makes me blush in time

In thought of the pursuit of so much moola, and I, like
Most of the sleepy earth, get to leap passed the monsters
For a while to help two small girls scale their beds after
Little prayers to tuck-in after the Hide-and-Seek cousins

Of Red Light-Green Light's and the Mother-May-I's to
Watch a simple gift, the fermented honey bee drink of
A *once upon* to release the busy day and, eventually
Hear the resting sound of deep, satisfied breathing

What You Keep

Existence was given you,
To print and publish and play,
To woodshed to perfection
The memories you hold,
To share their fragrance
With others, music you know,
Your illustrations within books,
Collaborations from cold
Chicago, that train-friendly
Town, to Italy with a romantic
Speech, *Bella Fortuna* your
Heartbeat, no matter where
You go, no matter whom you love;
Its metered rhythm holds the
Sounds you paint, your songs.

—for Jessie

Award winning poet Dan Pohl lives in Moundridge, Kansas, and instructs English composition at Hutchinson Community College. Pohl, along with his daughter Jessie, an artist who graduated from Bethel College (Newton, Kansas) in 2014, winner of the Thrasher Award for academic excellence, illustrates her father's works as well as children's books. In 2014, Pohl's book *Autochthonous: Found in Place* (Woodley Press), illustrated by Jessie, won The Nelson Poetry Book Award from The Kansas Authors Club. Pohl has appeared in many anthologies. You can find his works in *Begin Again: 150 Kansas Poems* (Woodley Press, 2013) and *To the Stars through Difficulties* (Mammoth Publications) both edited by past Kansas laureate, 2009-2013, Caryn Mirriam-Goldberg.   Recent anthologies include *365 Days: A Poetry Anthology* (365 Days Poetry, 2016 – edited by Roy Bekemeyer, James Benger, Dan Pohl, and Diane Wahto), as well as *Gimme Your Lunch Money: Heartland Poets Speak Out against Bullies* (Paladin Contemporaries) 2016 – edited by Dennis Etzel, Jr. and Lindsey Martin-Bowen. Many of Pohl's works can be found online, starting with kansaspoets.com. Jessie Pohl resides in Kansas City interacting with its art community.

This project was made possible, in part, by generous support from the Osage Arts Community.

Osage Arts Community provides temporary time, space and support for the creation of new artistic works in a retreat format, serving creative people of all kinds — visual artists, composers, poets, fiction and nonfiction writers. Located on a 152-acre farm in an isolated rural mountainside setting in Central Missouri and bordered by ¾ of a mile of the Gasconade River, OAC provides residencies to those working alone, as well as welcoming collaborative teams, offering living space and workspace in a country environment to emerging and mid-career artists. For more information, visit us at www.oac.com

Osage Arts Community

www.ingramcontent.com/pod-product-compliance
Lightning Source LLC
Chambersburg PA
CBHW021449080526
44588CB00009B/768